Negro Colored Black African

OH THE SHAME!

RITCHIE MAC

Negro, Colored, Black, African Oh the Shame! Copyright © 2015 by Ritchie Mac.

All rights reserved. Printed in the United States of America. No part of this book may be used or reproduced in any manner whatsoever without written permission except in the case of brief quotations embodied in critical articles or reviews.

This book is a work of non-fiction. However, names, characters, businesses, organizations, places, events and incidents either are the product of the author's imagination or are used fictitiously. Any resemblance to actual persons, living or dead, events, or locales is entirely coincidental.

For information contact: info@uptownmediaventures.com

Book and Cover design by Team Uptown

ISBN: 978-1-68121-011-7

First Edition: March, 2015

10 9 8 7 6 5 4 3 2 1

This book is dedicated to the memory of the late El Hajj Malik Shabazz, a.k.a. Malcolm X. His personal journey through life and the sincere transformation he made along the way is a daily inspiration for me personally.

I also feel that he does not receive the proper recognition he deserves for at least attempting to create unity among Afro Americans, as he wished to be called, and eventually equality among people of all ethnicities before his tragic and premature death.

The fact that any Afro American may have contributed to his death and seeing as this hate among each other continues to destroy Afro Americans today, is the driving force behind this book.

One Love to all people from every nation, tribe and tongue. Remember we all have at least one thing in common: Africa.

Page left intentionally blank

Chapters	Page
Introduction	7
Chapter 1 The Blacker the Berry	9
Chapter 2 The Life of a Brown Paper Bag Passing Negro	13
Chapter 3 Building Our Own Modern Day Slave Ship	19
Chapter 4 Our Love for Willie Lynch	23
Chapter 5 Trying to Own Everything Yet Owning Nothing	33
Chapter 6 First Step to Resolution is Acknowledgement	37
Chapter 7 Stop Supporting the Foolishness	41
Chapter 8 Attempting to Erase Your Skin Doesn't Make You Less black	47
Chapter 9 Crabs in a Barrel	53
Chapter 10 The Victim	57
Chapter 11 Stop Enabling Our Men to Act Like Women	63
Chapter 12 Use Your History to Empower You, Not to Enslave	67
Chapter 13 AIDS is Very Real!	71
Chapter 14 Going Back to Africa	77
Chapter 15 It Takes a Village	81
Chapter 16 At the End of the Day	85

Introduction

This book is the raw truth. There will be those who will hate it and those who will love it. There will be those who will argue about it and those who will talk about it. There will also be those who ignore it as if the issues don't affect them or somehow will go away.

But what everyone must realize is that the problem will exist no matter how each person reacts, unless we decide to stop complaining and start resolving our issues in our communities between our people. We will never find the level of peace, happiness or respect that we seek from others until we learn to deal with each other peaceably, until we learn to be happy with ourselves, and until we learn to respect one another whether we agree or disagree.

The book is written in general terms but it in no way is meant to generalize or to apply anything to every single person. I hope this book can create a small start in the resolution of a large problem.

One Love to you all!

Chapter 1
The Blacker the Berry

The color brown, no matter the shade, brings a lot of anger to the people inside of this skin. This is understandably so, as society has told them how ugly they are and has stereotyped the very people who were the victims of the people stereotyping themselves.

Of course being a black person in America seems to be less of a privilege than more. It hits home every day when we read the papers and watch the news, that blacks are less than welcome around others.

There's one really big problem with the above paragraph. I'm describing the behaviors within the black communities toward one another. Is there a question of what I'm saying? I will be glad to clarify. There is this intense hatred between the dark skinned and the light skinned blacks. People often have the misconception that the darker skin picks on the lighter skin only. This behavior is not exclusive to darker skin. Let's talk about the hatred shown to the darker skinned people.

I have heard the very fair skinned blacks speak very negatively of the darker skinned blacks. I have heard lighter skinned black people refer to darker skinned black people as ugly, crispy, baboon, ape, guerilla, African booty scratcher, and a few more. This is nothing new sadly. Videos show only the very light and biracial black women dancing around. No matter how obviously degrading these videos have become, the message sent to dark women is that they are not beautiful enough. Magazine covers have only very recently begun to show the faces of darker women. This did not just happen without a long fight.

What exactly is this "good hair" that people speak of? Why is this good hair only referred to when speaking of light skinned people? Do only dark people have nappy hair? Is nappy hair bad hair? Let's understand something. Good hair is healthy hair. Let's also understand that dark skinned people have authentic long soft baby fine hair too. And light skinned people have nappy hair too. The only bad hair is hair that is not healthy. But ignorant people fail to realize this simple fact.

What usually happens in the world of dating and even marriage? The light skinned women get chosen over the dark skinned women. I see it all too often these days. The whiter the skin, the prouder the man! Unless the dark skinned woman has an exceptional figure or a lot to offer financially, she is usually overlooked. The more nappy her hair is and the more fuller her lips are, in other words the more Afrocentric her features are, the much less desirable she is by her own people. An enormous insult to a dark person is telling them that they are handsome or beautiful "to be so dark." REALLY?

The dark male catches hell from his own people in ways that rip our families apart day by day. When the dark man succeeds at something great and removes himself from the negative environment that plagues the black communities, he is often ostracized. Many times he is called gay for speaking proper English and dressing in a more professional manner. If he chooses not to lead a "player" lifestyle people assume he is a homosexual. He is referred to as an Uncle Tom for speaking out against the things that go on in the inner cities among blacks.

This creates a great challenge for the men who are not as mentally strong or confident. Sadly, a lot of our men turn to the life of crime just to be acceptable to his people. This type of negativity is not as common among the light skinned black man because he is almost expected to succeed because of the advantages that he has for being light.

This causes a lot of anger that other ethnicities may not be aware of. This causes a whole lot of tension and creates a hopeless atmosphere that gives the feeling that if you can't catch a break from the inside, you certainly have no chance on the outside. Because of these intense feelings of eminent failure, a lot of our people fail to see the world for what it really has to offer.

They fail to see that everyone is not the enemy. But in their minds it is sort of the same as a parent constantly called their child stupid. No matter how much the teacher

Negro Colored Black African OH THE SHAME!

from the outside says that they are smart and gives them opportunities for advancement in the classroom, if the child's own parents tell them constantly that they are stupid, chances are that they will believe the parent and began to behave according to how they feel about themselves. This is what we create in our own communities but we keep on asking, "Why"?

Chapter 2
The Life of a Brown Paper Bag Passing Negro

This is the part that I can personally relate to. This is the part that affects me to this day. This is the part of being a black person that makes some gravitate toward other cultures and ethnicities and sometimes almost exclusively. I'm speaking of the light skinned watered down black person.

As a light skinned multiethnic black woman I can say that light skinned people are not very welcome in a lot of black communities. We are not the jokes of the communities, we are the enemies of the communities. The lighter the skin the more we are associated with being white. Even if we don't have any immediate Caucasian blood in us, our skin still serves as a reminder that we are an enemy to our own people.

We are also called a lot of degrading names. We hear things such as half bread, high yellow, zebra, oreo, watered down and many more names. We are often times labeled as being stuck up. The sad part is that a lot of light skinned blacks are as described as shown by their behaviors against

Negro Colored Black African OH THE SHAME!

our dark people in the first chapter. But most of us are not. So many times people tried to fight me or cause harm to me simply because of my skin color. You see, being light is also associated somehow with being weak.

Often times, people have the misconception that white people are weak so they link being light with being white and being weak.

Often times it is not safe being lighted skinned in our own communities. We are targets for bullies because people assume we are weak. It's sad but a lot of us find more love and comfort, and even acceptance, from Caucasians than we find from our own people.

What's also sad is that we are constantly reminded that we are not black enough, but if we dare to show any pride in our other half, we are angrily reminded that we are black and sometimes called sell outs because we equally love and acknowledge our other half. Some people seek love from blacks so much that they fail to acknowledge and may even deny their other half. I think it's truly heartbreaking.

We are not allowed to share the adversities that we face within our black communities because we are privileged in the eyes of our dark brothers and sisters so we have no right to complain at all. The same people who hurt us are the ones who swear that they have never seen a light skinned person catch a bad break. They fail to realize that our own people are the ones hurting us and kicking us out.

Again, there are those who have a snotty attitude

because they are light, but the majority of us are struggling and humbled and the hatred we receive from within hurts, even causing a great deal of resentment.

We did not ask to be born light and bi or multiracial. We asked for our lighter skin no more than anyone asked for their darker skin. Again, we are not made fun of, we are HATED by our own people. I speak so passionately about the light skinned blues because I live this every single day.

I have been threatened to have my face sliced so I won't think I'm too cute anymore. I have been threatened to have my hair cut off. I have been falsely accused of trying to flirt with or steal men from their women. I have been called arrogant for standing up for myself. I have been told that I don't speak black enough. Too many people have told me that I speak like a white girl so I'm not black enough and then laughed. People have tried to provoke me so they can fight me for no reason.

My own daughter has been a victim because of her extremely light skin and grayish green eyes and curly hair. She has been jumped coming off of the bus by a gang of dark girls. She has been relentlessly teased. Rumors have been spread about her that are hurtful. She has also been provoked. But you know something? Her friends to the end, who have never gone against her, come from her other side.

Now if she were to shout out her Latina pride in herself and her people who show her love she would really be hated. She would be denying her blackness somehow. No matter how many people want to say this isn't the truth, they can't change the fact that it is the truth.

It is a shame that in the secular world light skinned blacks do receive the longer end of the stick. We will land a position first even if we are less qualified than one of our dark skinned brothers or sisters. What most people fail to realize is that we didn't ask to be born in a world that sadly favors one skin color over the other. What people also fail to realize is that no matter what "light privileges" we may have extended to us and no matter what end of the stick we may usually receive, we are still just another nigger in this country.

Our light skin does not make us any less black in America. I don't care how we are mixed up and what contributes to our lightness, we are still and will always be just another nigger in this country. It doesn't matter how much more love we may be shown from others we are still niggers at the end of the day. It is hurtful though, that a lot of us feel more like niggers around our own people.

What I find amazing is that, much like myself, people who are light skinned do not always possess European features. I personally have very light eyes, my skin is significantly more colored than it's natural almost albino like color, because of my warm geographical location, and my hair is not exactly nappy. However I have a broad nose, very full lips and the back of my multi textured hair is soft but also as kinky as it wants to be.

I am nowhere near alone in possessing these Afrocentric features although I am multiracial through maternal blood immediately. This "other" blood is not from generations back but begins with my mother who is an Afro Hispanic Latina.

Let's be very clear about something. Spanish people share the African blood, some more than others, but nonetheless. To be more specific, the Hispanic comes from any group of Spanish people with dominant bloodlines of European, African and Native American. The Latino comes from predominant bloodlines of European and Native American. My mother falls under both. Hence the very proud label of Afro Hispanic Latina and I will shout my Hispanic Latina pride to the moon and back, the same as I do my Afro pride.

However this is another subject in another book. My father is "African American," for the sake of argument. I take issue with that label. I doubt that too many blacks in American are actually African American, but that's also another subject in another book.

Amazingly though, there are an overwhelming amount of dark skinned blacks who have more narrow noses and skinnier lips than Europeans themselves. Their skin may be dark and very often their hair is natural nappy, but they have less Afrocentric facial features than their light skinned brothers and sisters like me. They are BEAUTIFUL.

The females don't need all of the makeup to cover up their flawless skin. Oftentimes their skin compliments the

Negro Colored Black African OH THE SHAME!

makeup and not the other way around. But they don't see it. Our light skin still makes us targets for hatred no matter what our features look like.

We have this color war, against us, among ourselves. It's sad that people are made to feel inferior or ugly or weak because of the skin that they were not asked to be born into. The words Negro, Colored, Black and African are looked upon as something shameful or inferior by our own people. because of this diseased mentality.

I would like to talk about how we contribute to our own demise and how we perpetuate the stereotypes that others have against us.

Chapter 3
Building Our Own Modern Day Slave Ship

Picture this scenario: Three young males walk into an upscale department store. They each have their underwear showing as their pants are literally being held by a belt against the very bottom of their backsides. Everyone else is dressed very casual but classy.

The voice levels are very low - almost at a whisper. While everyone shops around, one of the young males yells out to a worker, "What the fuck you lookin' at bitch?" The other young males began speaking loudly saying, "Yeah my nigga I know, I'll go off in this mug on these muthafuckas."

Almost instantly a security guard approaches the men. The security officer is threatened with physical violence. A scuffle takes place and the three men jump on the one security officer. Law enforcement now intervenes and one of the young males is critically injured.

Let's stop here for a moment. Now let's say that a worst case scenario is the result of this incident. Who is to blame? Is it an officer who shot at one of the young males for sticking his hand in his pocket when the police told them to put their hands in the air? Is it the young males who entered the department store verbally abusing a worker? We can say that a police officer is the wrong one for shooting an unarmed man? But we must ask some questions before we dismiss the rest of the story.

The problem I have is that our young men already know that they have a million strikes against them just because they are black. They already know that most of our men are unjustifiably profiled. So then, why do so many of our men behave in ways that they know will draw negative attention? Why are we as a people so shocked when we hear the aggressive and even violent actions behind tragic stories like this one? I don't understand why we keep asking ourselves why no one wants to move next door to us or why no one wants to hire us.

Another example is the angry female behind the cash register. Or the angry female at the bank or in any customer service related job. I personally find myself wanting to go into another line because our women always have such attitudes for no reason. It is such a problem that it makes a person almost want to generalize.

Our women are not good with customer service. Of course I know not to generalize because then this would include me. But for a very large part, in my personal experiences and those stated by a lot of others, there is this anger. It seems to be a generalized anger toward everything and everyone.

There was a time when I was in the grocery store. I was

pretty upset at the high prices of the produce. There happened to be a Caucasian woman examining her fruit next to me so I decided to mention how ridiculous the cost of produce was. She agreed and this started a conversation. Soon two other Caucasian women joined in the conversation so we began to share different ways on how to save on produce.

There was a black woman who came over toward us. She actually seemed pretty upset at the cost of grapes verses the amount of grapes in the bag. So I kindly said to her, "Isn't that ridiculous that the price is so high yet you barely get any grapes?" She looked at me, turned her lip up, rolled her eyes, and walked away. I was taken aback.

Now here I was able to have a productive small conversation among those who are supposed to hate me because I'm not white, yet my "sista'" just dogged me pretty heavy for absolutely no reason at all. Am I supposed to feel closer to my people?

This seemingly pure hatred with black women for one another has been going on since I was a teenager in my life. When I'm in a store or walking down the street, the women either bump me as if they're looking for a fight or they laugh and say something smartass.

I sure have threatened a few and I was ready to fight in my younger days. All but one was squashed once I stood up for myself. As an adult now, if I sense that someone may do something ignorant I just move out of the way because it's insane at this point in life to fight over nothing, or too much of anything for that matter.

So, here we have these examples of our behaviors and we seem to never know why people avoid us. We are mean to ourselves. We belittle ourselves at any sign of advancement within. We feel like it's a betrayal for one of us to move out of our run down drug infested communities. We put any description of ourselves into this box.

There is this thing called "acting black." How does a black person act? We complain when others stereotype us yet we stereotype ourselves.

Do we realize that we put chains on ourselves in this society? The pride that we should have is taken from our own, by our own. The same way slaves were taken from their loved ones is the same way we take love from ourselves.

We no longer need to police, the KKK, or any other white supremacy group to kill us off. We kill one another and seemingly with pride.

We refuse to leave the slave ship. We refuse to stop labeling one another as the house or field nigga. We are building our own modern day slave ship. Do you want to know what's really sad?

Chapter 4
Our Love for Willie Lynch

Nothing would make Lynch more proud than to know that his plan to divide and conquer us has been so effective that we actually trick ourselves into believing that the word nigger could ever become a term of endearment among ourselves.

We actually trick our own minds into believing that just because we change the spelling and pronunciation a bit, that "nigga" no longer means nigger. Some people say their "kids" are in elementary school. Some people say their "children" are in elementary school. Completely different spelling and pronunciation but it means the exact same thing. That's how I compare the words nigger and nigga.

Let's talk about how we love to keep Willie alive with this divide and conquer mentality. We have already discussed how the light skin verses the dark skin affects our people. Now let's talk about the men against the women. This is the part that causes the high rate of single parenthood.

Our men find our women especially hard to get along with. They allege that black women are too negative. We nag too much and talk too much. We are alleged gold diggers. We allegedly only see men for the amount of money he has and what material possessions he has to show for.

They say that we are not supportive whenever they do try to elevate themselves. We tear them down with harsh words. If our men do have a job but its low paying, we belittle his manhood and we make him feel less than a man.

They also say that they have grown tired of seeing our women wearing hair extensions, false colored eyes, and anything else not naturally belonging to us.

Now of course this statement cannot be generalized because I most certainly do not fit into this category in any way. There are a whole lot of black women who don't fit into this category in any way. But nevertheless this is what a whole lot of black men complain that black women do. We have to address this issue.

They all couldn't be completely wrong. And perhaps the majority of our men do want to see our women appear more natural and wear our hair in its natural state. This doesn't mean that they all are correct or feel this way either. But let's say that they are correct. Let's examine what the ladies have to say about the men.

Our women feel that our men have no real sense of family. When we examine men from other cultures and ethnicities we see the men providing homes for his wife and children. We see these men moving the women into THEIR homes. We see the men with careers. Our women see our men also as gold diggers. They come into our lives to use us and not to love us. Sometimes we don't know why our men are with us because they also put us down so badly. We are forever compared to females of other races.

Again the dark and the light women are played against each other. Our men seem to always look for excuses not to advance. The white man and society are always at fault but responsibility is never taken for their own behaviors. There are way too many homes where the men are using the women's car and using the woman's money. Our men seem to run as fast as they can from being a father to their children. We have no leadership from our men in our community.

If we were to remove the hair weaves and go natural, which for many of our sisters would be kinky or nappy shorter hair, our men would turn their lips up and tell us how unattractive natural black women are. They would complain that nappy hair is just plain ugly then they would proceed to date a woman with a weave or with naturally straighter hair.

Black men hardly ever support or love a sister that decides to go natural. Black men only praise a black woman's natural state if her hair is naturally soft and curly or if her skin is light. Our men make our women feel ugly. They make us feel like we are the ugliest group of women among the rest.

Now a few things need to be examined here. Ladies, remember my rant about the attitudes that a LOT of our women have? Well this may be what our men are talking about.

That general anger that is carried around will drag the most optimistic individual down almost into a depressed state of being. If we can't make our men feel understood, respected, loved, and appreciated for what they do and sincerely attempt to do, they won't like us much.

It's that simple. If no one believes in them from the inside then they feel no one will believe in them period. We are their backbones. Our men have every strike imaginable, against them because of the skin they never asked to be born into. They are frustrated. They need the homes that we provide for them to be a haven - not a hell whole.

Gentlemen, however, you must realize that our women are tired. We are tired of playing the role of the mother and father. We are tired of being called ugly and less attractive than everyone else.

Sometimes we yell at our men because we see other black men succeed, but nowhere near enough, so we yell in order to get the attention of the many men who behave as children. We are tired of video games babysitting our men.

We have had enough of forever providing for our men and holding our men up while we are used and torn down. We may put great emphasis on the money that our men make at times because we know when they are capable of more. We have had enough of our men dividing us up according to light and dark or so called good hair and nappy hair. We are tired of competing for the attention and love and acceptance of our black men.

We have watched our men go from the greats of Malcolm X, Martin Luther King Jr., and the likes; to rappers that degrade our women, men who dress as women, and men who don't know if they want to be a man or a woman.

Our men are undercover homosexuals in record numbers. Brothers, we have held our hurting men down for so long but with little reciprocity lately. It's hard to respect a man's headship when we are often the heads of the homes. We find that difficult to respect. Brothers, WE ARE TIRED.

Both sides are guilty. But do you see how Willie Lynch planned this so perfectly? It's probably more successful than he would have imagined it to be. I don't think Willie had any idea in his mind that someday we would have broken free from the chains of the slavery that was inflicted upon us.

Our men and women have so much resentment toward one another that we keep our children being born in a perpetual state of dysfunction. Our kids seem to view single parent homes as normal. We as adults seem to view single parenthood as the better option at times, in order to avoid the feelings that we have toward each other.

Our men were trained to be physically strong but emotionally weak. Our women were trained to see weak men and not be able to rely on them. I truly feel that our men want to try harder. I know they do, but they have not unlearned the slave trained mind even though they have themselves never been slaves - except of their own minds.

I know our women love our men. We want to believe in you brothers, we really do. But when you don't believe in yourselves we carry that weight on us. We are left to pick up every peace that you leave. Some sisters may be so angry because they are exhausted. This is no excuse for bad behaviors towards those who do no wrong to them but this is a root cause of general bad attitudes. However those attitudes make our men run from us.

The problem will continue to exist as long as we continue to love Willie Lynch and his training manual for our people.

We keep our chains of slavery as tight as ever when we openly disrespect our own people. Calling one another "niggas," no matter how acceptable someone told us this is, has not and never will gain the respect we seek from others. Respect is not just given, it must be earned.

No one takes us seriously when we burn down our already ailing communities when an injustice has been committed against one of our people. There is absolutely no logic in this behavior at all. It keeps the stereotypes of destructive and animalistic black people, going. No one wants to be neighbors with people who think it's cool to be a bad ass every day. We don't want to be neighbors with our own people for the very same reasons.

We are angry. If we ourselves know that we are angry, other people certainly know that we are angry. We seem to relieve our anger in violent ways so many times. We kill one another just because someone looked at us wrong. Instead of protesting peacefully, we decide to loot and destroy our own communities.

It doesn't matter that others join in because their problems are still different than ours. It matters that we participate in this behavior at all. We get upset and complain of other people putting cheap businesses in the same neighborhoods that we reside in but refuse to build up. We spend all of our money making everyone else rich.

We have Africans that come to this country with nothing but the clothing on their backs and somehow they manage to own corporations. They look at the so called "African American" in utter disbelief because they cannot comprehend why we don't take advantage of the opportunities given to us.

It doesn't matter that our people may receive the shorter end of the stick. It matters that we have any part of that stick and the ability and opportunities to extend that stick ourselves.

There was a period in time when the only stick our people felt was the one beaten against their skin among other objects. We have too many excuses and no solutions. We throw pity parties for our people as we watch others advance. But we always ask, "Why?"

No one takes our people seriously because we don't take ourselves seriously. No one respects us because we disrespect ourselves. There is often a cost to pay when someone disagrees with another. There is no such thing as agreeing to disagree. We do everything to make another's life miserable when we are angry with them.

Social media is the Devil's pit. We use social media not only to put all of our own business out for everyone to see, but we use it to completely dismantle any level of dignity or peace that another person might have.

We call one another the most degrading names. We spread all kinds of rumors in an effort to bring complete misery to a person we may be angry with. We use social media to spew all of the hatred and evil that is in our hearts. We make mountains out of mole hills. We prefer to use the public comment section to talk all the crap we can to a person instead of approaching the issue via personal message.

We say a lot of stuff that most would not say to a person's face, ever. People get bold on social media and they show just how evil they really are. They show how unreasonable and angry they really are.

The minute a person speaks on the negative behaviors of our people, the minute everyone calls this person a coon, an Uncle Tom' or a sellout; somehow they are kissing the ass of the white man and loving the slave master. What slave master? Is this the master that has our people standing in line to buy hundred dollar shoes? Is this the master that has our people caring more about buying fancy cars that are often repossessed eventually and "bling" instead of investing their money into education and homes to own? Is this the master that has our people putting money into the pockets of those we deem our enemies while we surpass every opportunity to own our own businesses? Is this the master that forces us to divide ourselves by the color of our skin? Is this the master who we see looking back at us when we stare in the mirror?

In that case I'd say they have more love for the slave master than their own people. We are the ones enslaving ourselves and those who speak against the problems that we inflict on ourselves are only trying to save us from the slavery of our own minds.

Yes we are the masters of ourselves. We are the masters that keep our own minds and our own people enslaved. Until we can admit that we are still slaves. We will remain slaves and no one will respect us until we respect ourselves as a people.

Break the chains!

Chapter 5
Trying to Own Everything Yet Owning Nothing

A young twelve year old Caucasian girl took a verbal beating from the black communities for wearing boxed braids. I read about this situation on social media and googled the article to make sure it was legit. Social media at times spews false venom so I always check for the legitimacy of the stories I read.

I was beyond disappointed. Here we have a twelve year old girl who is being told that she is mocking black people because she is wearing boxed braids. Then there were others complaining that white people are always trying to steal anything that black people can call their own, to further steal their pride and identity, and they disguise their evil by pretending that they actually admire the styles and music that they steal from us.

Are these people serious? It's hard to even entertain this nonsense with a response but I will try.

I will start with a question. Would this same logic apply to our sisters who wear European textured hair extensions, blond colored hair, and blue contact lenses? Would this in any way suggest that perhaps our sisters are trying to be "white" or steal the appearance of a white person? Does this question sound pitiful? It should, because it is.

It is that much more pitiful to attack a child because she really thinks that braids are cute.

Somehow people also have an issue with Caucasian hip hop artists. They feel that they are stealing something that belongs to blacks. Even when someone is obviously talented and in many ways more talented than their black peers, they are put down and called lame.

Eminem comes to my mind immediately. People are not happy when artists like Iggy Azalea come into the industry and actually make a lot of money. But what about artists like Hootie and the Blowfish, Tracy Chapman, Seal, and other black artists that lean more towards "contemporary white American" music? Are they trying to be white or steal the style of white people?

Have we become so closed minded that we must book music into a box right along with our stereotypes of ourselves? Good music can't be universal? Must we label music the same way we cry that people label us?

I never understood why being black supposedly came with a certain look and attitude. Perhaps this label that we put on ourselves is what causes so many of us to have unpleasant attitudes. Perhaps so many of us feel that being black means being tough so this is the attitude that we carry around daily and this is why other people have such a hard time getting along with us or even trusting us for that matter. But why do we do this to ourselves?

Are we so insecure that we somehow remain delusional in thinking that we live in a cotton field with a bullwhip over us? Do we picture ourselves still so helpless that we put up this front of being mean and tough as a defense mechanism to protect ourselves in a country that still beats us? Have we not noticed yet that we kill ourselves more than the so-called oppressor these days? Who will be the first to remove their heads from the sand of oblivion? Who will be the first to stop labeling everything so that others may perhaps stop labeling us?

We do not own any music. Whoever created the various songs are the owners of the music and I'm sure they would not want to limit their audience to any group of people.

But there is a bigger issue that has to do with ownership. Why don't we own any of the businesses in our neighborhoods? Why are we so hell bent about claiming ownership of all of the things that are not ours to begin with such as music, fashion, or attitudes, but we are idle when it comes to ownership of something that we really can benefit from that will generate wealth and help us all?

I will never understand how our people complain about the Middle Easterners and the Asians that create wealth in our communities because we most certainly buy from them.

In fact we are their greatest source of income. From the clothing, to the accessories, to the hair products, we love to make our Asians rich. From the food to the electronics we

Negro Colored Black African OH THE SHAME!

love to make our Middle Easterners rich, and you know what? I'm not mad at them at all. In fact I respect them for doing what they have to do to make money because they are not selling drugs or shooting our people as we do to ourselves.

They are simply making money and we are their greatest allies when it comes to generating wealth, whether we mean to be or not.

To be quite honest, I have had only one incident, to date, of an Asian following me around in their store. Otherwise I have always had very respectful and even pleasant encounters with the Asians.

I have Middle Easterners in my family so once again I have had very enriching and family-like relationships with Middle Easterners. The bottom line is that you usually get respect when you give it. Not always, but more so than not.

I want to see the beginning of businesses being built in our communities by our people. I'd love to see the black communities try hard to claim ownership of businesses instead of hip hop music or hair styles and the likes.

I'd also love to see our people create wealth together without behaving like crabs in a barrel. We need to stop being jealous of one another and learn to encourage and uplift one another. We sound foolish arguing over ownership of music when we don't own anything of importance in our own backyard.

Chapter 6

The First Step to Resolution is Acknowledgement

We accept responsibility when we acknowledge the issues. It is all of our responsibility to acknowledge the problems even if we feel we don't behave in certain ways and even if we feel we have advanced far enough that it doesn't affect us.

We must not lie to ourselves. Light or dark, mixed immediately or from generations back, if you have any significant or noticeable African blood in you, you are affected, period.

It amazes me and angers me how I see our people recalling all of the atrocities that took place in slavery and during the civil rights movements towards our people; but for some reason when someone brings out the exact same actions that we commit against ourselves somehow everyone has an excuse.

It is deemed racists for people who are not black, to point out the violence that we commit against our own people. It is called being a coon or an Uncle Tom when our own people point out the violence that we commit against ourselves.

Negro Colored Black African OH THE SHAME!

It's the exact same principle that applies to AA participants. The first step to recovering from alcoholism is to acknowledge that you are an alcoholic. Change is not possible where there is no acknowledgement.

So this is why this step of acknowledging the issues in our communities, paramount in order for us to talk about solutions? We have to stop being so afraid to say that something is wrong. We have to stop pretending that these issues do not affect us all just because we may not behave in a certain manner or just because we have the opportunities to advance ourselves in a way that others may not have.

Even if you are not directly surrounded by the issues that I mentioned in the previous chapters you are still affected because a lot of people tend to stereotype our people based upon the behavior of a lot of our people in our communities.

Acknowledgement of the issues in our communities is not an admittance that we somehow personally contribute to the downfall of our people, but pretending the issues don't affect us or pretending that the issues don't exist is actually a contribution to the continued downfall of our people.

We have to stop pointing fingers to the "white man." He is not doing the "drive-bys" on our people. He is not forcing our people to join gangs and kill one another in the name of loyalty or "being down." He is not forcing our people to sell drugs in our communities to one another. He is not the one killing our people over social media disagreements or over a look that someone gives us. He is not the one putting our people on hit lists because he feels disrespected in some way.

We already know the strikes against our people from the other side. They have no problem admitting to their feelings about us and they definitely have no problems showing us how they feel. We know who our enemies are on the other side so we have the advantage of being forewarned and behaving accordingly.

We become our own worst enemies when we smile at each other with hate in our hearts. That's the real danger to us, not them. When we can admit that there are self-hate issues in our communities and self-esteem issues among our people in countless numbers, then we can work toward resolution. Until then we will always be the victim. We will always be in the back seat, so to speak.

Chapter 7
Stop Supporting the Foolishness

Crime in the inner cities is nothing new. This is an issue that is always met with an interesting response though. The reason why there is so much crime in the inner cities is because of lack of opportunities and financial stability. Our people resort to crime because they are frustrated and see no other way out. They become angry because life is so unfair.

These are the primary answers that are given when asked about the insane amount of crime in our communities.

I find these responses quite interesting though. Let's assume for a moment that a large portion of black celebrities started off in poverty. Let's assume that they too were once victims of the "inner city blues."

Well, this begs the question of why so many of our multimillionaire celebrities are still getting into trouble with the law and acting out in ways that are compatible to the actions of those who complain that lack of money is the reason for their misbehaviors.

It further concerns me that we have become so immune

to the stereotypes and treatment of our people that we actually have begun to accept these behaviors and actually deem them appropriate.

What exactly am I talking about? Let's look at the rap music. Violence, drugs, partying, and degradation of our women is what sells. These topics are what make these young rappers millionaires. More than likely, if someone were to rap about making a family, creating a business, loving your woman or anything positive; no matter how creative the words are and no matter how catchy the beat is, their song would not sell very well. It's boring. There's no drama.

I find it hard to comprehend how someone could be a multimillionaire, thus have the options to walk away from all of the inner city blues, but they still choose to go to parties where they know their enemies will be present. They carry their guns with them and they pretty much help to set up a violent evening.

But when they get caught then all of the excuses, that no longer apply to them, start flowing in. Somehow the white man is responsible for all the injustices that are about to take place against him inside of the courtroom. When is responsibility ever taken to stay out of trouble? Why are these behaviors even given airtime?

The problems that we face are not limited to those who are economically disadvantaged. It is much deeper than that. There is a hatred that our people feel for ourselves.

The anger that we direct toward the white man and any other group of people is actually a reflection of the anger that we feel toward ourselves.

We have been told that our people are only good for sports and physical labor, so we believe this nonsense and behave accordingly. We are told that our people are ugly and dark and the most unappealing race, so we believe this nonsense and behave accordingly. We are told that we are stupid and we believe this nonsense and we behave accordingly.

Have you ever stopped to think about how people belittle a person who they are jealous of? If for example, a woman sees another woman who is pleasing to look at, has a nice personality, has a husband who appears dedicated, well-kept children, and a successful career; thus another woman may become jealous.

As a result, rumors might start spreading. The rumors may be that the husband is being unfaithful. If this gets back to this beautiful young woman, she may begin to question her husband. Perhaps if she is told that she is ugly enough times, she may begin to feel self-conscious about her appearance. What if her well-mannered children are picked on for being good children? This may cause the children to begin acting out. Eventually all of this negativity will begin to rip the whole family apart all because of one or a few jealous people spreading false words from hatred and jealousy.

Negro Colored Black African OH THE SHAME!

This is exactly what our people need to consider when they recall all of the horrible things that were said about our people over the years. Perhaps there was a great deal of jealousy going on. Did you ever consider that being dark is a sign of strength? Did you ever consider that the nappy hair is a sign of uniqueness and it stands out from the rest of the world? Did you ever consider that our broad features are actually envied which is why everyone is getting lip injections to mimic our naturally full lips that have been criticized over the years?

Perhaps our strong physical strength also contributed to some of our many silenced inventions that actually take a SMART individual to invent. No one tells us these things for fear that we may actually succeed at taking over this nation. Did you think about that? Jealousy makes people say some ugly things. If a person hears it enough, they begin to believe these things and it's crippling, even paralyzing.

The sad thing is that we now accept the ugly things that were said about us, and we behave accordingly. Now, when people say we are killing ourselves off, it's the truth. Now, when people say we have nasty attitudes, it's the truth. Now, when people say we behave as uneducated people, unfortunately for a large enough part, it is the truth. What's really sad is that these young thuggish acting individuals actually have college degrees. They are extremely intelligent but they prefer to behave stupidly.

We must stop supporting the foolishness. It is not ok for

us the cheer on these rappers as they further degrade our people with pride. It is not ok to ignore the drugs coming through our communities by our own people. It is totally inappropriate to accept and speak improper English because we believe it is the "black" thing to do.

Just because it is acceptable with seemingly everyone form every ethnicity, it is not appropriate for our men to sag their pants and lower their standards of appearance in the name of popularity.

What ever happened to holding the doors open for our elders and our women? What ever happened to putting on very nice clothing to go on a date or to the movies? Whatever happened to our women wearing natural and attractive hair colors that compliment us and not cause distraction? Why have we decided to lower our standards over the decades?

Take a look back to the days of our civil rights leaders. They were being shot, lynched, burned alive, bitten by dogs, sprayed around by fire hoses, and anything else you can think of; for us to have the opportunities that we have today - yet they dressed so beautifully.

The women were breathtaking. The men were so handsome. This was not just the standard for "Hollywood" colored actors and actresses. This was the standard for even the poorest of the poor. Why is this no longer even acceptable? This is something we really need to think about.

Unfortunately in this society you are judged by your

Negro Colored Black African OH THE SHAME!

appearance. We have to stop accepting and supporting foolishness and elevate our standards to the way they used to be. That's how our people were able to get any kind of opportunity in this country. We set ourselves to high standards in our past; why stop now?

Chapter 8

Attempting to Erase Your Skin Doesn't Make You Less Black

All over the world today there are countless amounts of black people bleaching their skin and narrowing their noses in a pitiful attempt to appear "less black." Oh the shame!

"The man" has told you how ugly and bad your dark skin is and you believed him? Does your dark skin remind you of the slavery that you never experienced but love to use as a crutch anyways?

While you bleach your skin to appear lighter than the beautiful and powerful skin that you were born into, there are countless amounts of white and bright people around the world today "lying" under the sun trying to achieve the skin color that you deem a curse.

We are the only group of people who post pictures of black people around the world to shout to the world how beautiful our black is. That in itself is not a problem - it's the reason why we do it that concerns me. Those posts don't seem to come from a place of pride in my opinion. It seems as though this is an attempt to convince ourselves that our black is beautiful, but we still don't seem convinced.

Negro Colored Black African OH THE SHAME!

If you know that we are beautiful we don't need to say it over and over and over again. We post photos of our little girls with big earrings and make up just to tell the world that black is beautiful.

Why do we need to do this? What's understood and obvious needs no explanation, I promise.

What concerns me and saddens me are the Lil Kim's in the world. This is just one of the many examples of the hatred that so many of our people feel for themselves. What has she done to herself? She doesn't even appear human anymore. I wonder if she is unhappier now than what she was before she attempted to erase her blackness.

Of course we all know how much hatred Michael Jackson had for his blackness. Aside from his skin which may legitimately be from the skin disease vitiligo; but what about all of the nose jobs? When he passed on he barely had a nose. He had the surgeons to chisel away all of his Afrocentric features.

He was really a sad case of self-hatred to observe over the years. What about the March, 2015 issue of *In Style* magazine where Kerry Washington graces the cover? If you have not seen it you should take a look. Ms. Washington does not look like herself at all. She appears at least two and a half shades lighter than her original.

Should we be upset about this? Well, I'd say it is definitely a cause for concern because this hatred for self is a large part of the reason why I am writing this book at all.

This is the reason why we have so much division among our people right now.

We divide ourselves by skin color more than anything. So yes it is an enormous cause for concern because no matter what shade of brown you are, this mindset affects you in one way or another.

What we seem to have here is an extended field and house negro mentality. Somehow our minds went back to the plantations. This time, however, it is not the white slave masters dividing us by the color of our skin, it is our own people continuing the legacy of hatred and dividing and conquering. As long as we categorize one another according to skin color we will continue to hate one another and to kill one another.

Let's shed some light on how we can resolve this hatred or this overindulgence of the skin that we are in. I want to start with the house slave mentality. I said it and I'll say it again, there are a lot of light skinned and even pale skinned blacks who honestly feel like they are superior to those with darker skin.

The reason they feel this way is because of the privileges that may have been and often times are extended to those with lighter skin. Unfortunately we live in a world where favoritism is shown in many forms and unfortunately one of those forms is with skin color.

Let me make it clear that blacks are not the only group of people who have issues with skin color division but we will stick to the subject of the issues with blacks for now.

We live in a society where the majority rules even if it's wrong unfortunately. But this can be and needs to start being used to our advantage. To the blacks with the house negro mentality, who think that their skin color makes them better than the rest:

Stop it!

The more you perpetuate this behavior the more the rest of society will also continue to divide our people. When you start to realize that you are not the white mans' favorite, maybe you will start to treat your darker brothers and sisters with respect.

When you realize that no matter how many privileges you may have in this country, at the end of the day you are still a nigger in this country, perhaps you will start to respect your darker brothers and sisters.

It is not ok to make fun of a person with blue black skin or any other shade of darkness. It is not ok to assume that everyone should be jealous of you because your skin is closer to white. It is not ok to join the ranks of ignorant people who make insulting comments such as, "they are good looking to be so dark."

I hear this nonsense all the time. I'm putting it all out there. As I stated earlier on, most light skinned blacks are not conceited. Most of us actually wish we felt more inclusive with our people. But because of the few whom do treat darker skin as lesser than lighter shades, we all catch the wrath of those who may fall victim to this ignorant behavior.

The way that we treat one another does affect us all. Be mindful of this the next time you or someone you know laughs at the color of a person's dark skin or mentions how nappy a person's hair is.

Now I'm speaking to my dark skinned brothers and sisters.

The dark skinned slaves who were kept in the field for being dark were not insignificant and neither are you. You were never a slave to anyone except your own minds. Stop being the victim. You are not a victim. Stop letting stupid people make you feel like you are insignificant because perhaps they fear the power that you really have.

People want you to keep living in hatred and fear because they know that if you overcome this mindset, you will prove how powerful you are and this takes the spotlight off of your oppressors and it gives you recognition that you deserve.

People will treat you how you allow them to treat you. Females, when you see a light skinned woman walk past you, stop giving the insecure dirty looks. Walk past, smile and keep your head up because you are beautiful, literally!

It's the attitudes that takes away from the beauty, that you fear you don't have. Men, light skin is not in style. To me, the sexiest sight to behold is a dark brother, with his head held up high, dressed in a suit and taking care of his business. You have to have confidence.

Stop making light skinned people feel like they are not black enough and stop assuming that we are weak. We are all in this together. No matter how recent our mixture is we are still black.

The truth is that when light skinned people use their skin color as a weapon, it just shows how ashamed they are of their blackness. Some people will try to pull off being another ethnicity just to alleviate the shame that they really feel inside for being black. The book cover of this book shows what dark skinned people are doing to show their self- hatred.

It begins with each individual. If each individual would take responsibility for his or her own actions, then we will see as a group of people, we will be much better united and we won't be so angry with one another and everyone else in the world.

We can't keep pointing fingers to the outside when we have so much hate for one another on the inside. People are sitting back laughing at this show we put on and it's getting old.

No one is better than the other and none of us are victims. The only person who makes you a victim is yourself.

Chapter 9

Crabs in a Barrel

Whenever someone tries to succeed there is always someone putting them down. If there were three black owned businesses and one white owned business on the same block, chances are the white owned business would succeed better than the three black businesses. We do not support one another.

I take notice to a whole lot of things and how people interact with one another on social media. Social media has opened my eyes to a lot of things that I'd rather not see but that I must be made aware of.

One of the examples of the crabs in a barrel mentality is shown when someone is trying to promote a legitimate business. No one seems to reply. But when that same person posts bad news or maybe something a bit dramatic, all kinds of feedback is received. If this person posts photos there are one hundred likes. But if a person is asking for likes to promote a business or information to support a cause, it remains silent.

There also seems to be a lot of competition and nowhere near enough support and teamwork. No one seems to comprehend the benefits that teamwork will have on our people and our communities as a whole. Instead of cheering someone on for gaining some financial ground, people will sit around and talk about how stupid this person's idea is. People will predict when this person will fail at their attempts to achieve financial success. Instead of helping one another, people will try to outshine one another and steal the spotlight.

There are those people who will almost sarcastically tell you that they are happy for you, but then that statement is always followed by a "but." They will then pretend to care enough about to you to warn you of all the things that may go wrong when their attempt is actually to cause doubt or discourage you from moving forward.

The crabs in a barrel mentality is not limited to financial situations. It also happens when people seek happiness and stability in their personal lives. When a person finds a mate that is positive and enhances their lives, people are looking for every reason why this relationship won't work out.

Females especially, tend to judge and criticize another female for having a man who may not seem to have an excessive amount of money. They don't point out the fact that the man is faithful and still takes care of his home financially and spiritually.

Men tend encourage one another not to settle down too much and they basically encourage one another to continue the "player" lifestyle although the person is now in a committed relationship or marriage with a good woman.

Beware of those who want to know every single detail about the person you're dating or that you marry. People will take what you say, twist it to their liking, and use it against you. Social media has people looking at one another's profile pictures and statuses just to see if the person is happy or not. They will report their findings to others. People cannot stand to see another person happy, especially when their own situation is bleak.

Truthfully, if a person was really happy in their own lives they would not have time to find reasons to be unhappy with someone else's. This is why it is important to keep your spousal disagreements off of the internet. It's also just tacky.

A lot of people rejoice in the failed relationships of others. Suddenly they become your friend. They pretend to show you comfort when really they are just so overjoyed that someone else is hurting, so they now have the energy to pretend to care about you. This makes them feel elevated and now able to outshine you. They don't realize that this mentality is contributing to the downfall of the black family and community. People are so ugly that they may even attempt to seduce or steal your mate.

There's always a reason to call someone a sellout when he is just trying to rise above his current situation. There is always a reason to call someone a coon or a "negropean" when he speaks proper English or doesn't allow past events against blacks to influence his actions and state of mind. There is always a reason to try to outshine someone with

Negro Colored Black African OH THE SHAME!

money, popularity or material things; just to make someone feel defeated.

Until we stop pushing each other down every time someone succeeds or at least attempts to succeed, we will never move forward or achieve anything major as blacks.

Chapter 10
The Victim

Do not forget that "we" were slaves. Do not minimize what slavery has done to "us." We will never be acceptable to white people. "We" deserve reparations for being slaves. The Jews never forgot about the Holocaust so why should we forget about slavery? What about the blacks that were exterminated along with the Jews? They don't ever tell you about that.

Here's the problem with these statements. "We" were never slaves. Our parents were also never slaves. More than likely none of our grandparents were slaves depending on your age. Why should "we" deserve reparations? The funny thing is that the people shouting these statements are mostly from the younger generations, so "we" weren't even around or barely old enough to recall any experiences of even the Civil Rights movements.

Most of the people shouting about "us" being slaves were small children or barely born when the Black Panthers were seriously in action. What do "we" possibly know about being slaves besides what we read and hear?

Do you want to know the VERY BIG DIFFERENCE between the Jews and ourselves?

Negro Colored Black African OH THE SHAME!

The Jews are aware of the holocaust and some actually remember the holocaust but they don't live life as if they are victims of the Holocaust. These people stick together better than anyone and they continue to build their communities, build wealth for their people, and look out for one another. They make sure that their people are always employed.

They make sure that their neighborhoods remain generally safe. When something looks out of place they act upon it rationally, yet proactively. They don't ask anyone to see them as victims. They don't remind everyone every chance that they get about the atrocities committed in the Holocaust, nor do they compare their history with the history of others to minimize the struggles of others while seeking sympathy for their struggles.

Why is this concept seemingly so hard for our people to comprehend? Isn't it obvious that playing the victim and continuously recalling the past, isn't getting us anywhere at all? We complain that the world still hates us so we must remind them of why they are evil for hating us.

We complain that we are not welcome nor wanted in society so we use slavery as a reason to tell our people why we must remain separate. I want to speak on an issue in particular that ruffles my feathers in regards to this whole victim role playing.

It bothers me and actually angers me when a white person adopts a black child and the entire black community gets into an uproar over it because now the child will not have the opportunity to learn about his culture and heritage. Not one person is in an uproar about why none of our own people are adopting black children. No one is in an uproar about why so many of our children are in foster care at all. Every excuse is made as to why underhanded white folks are really adopting black children. Well, let's assume for the moment that there is an agenda behind why a lot of white people adopt black children.

What are "we" doing about it? Would we rather see the child bounce from home to home instead of being in a stable home, just to avoid being raised by white folks? Have we really come to the level of bitterness that would allow us to feel more comfortable with a black child in foster care instead of a loving and stable residence full of white folks? Really?

Some people are going to hate me for this but I personally prefer general happiness any day. If a white person adopting a black child out of a horrible abusive foster care system and into a stable and loving environment, means that the child may not completely learn about the history of their ancestors and may not practice African culture, which by the way is not hardly practiced by any blacks in America, then I'm all for it!

Until someone can tell me what we practice in black American culture that connects us in any meaningful way to Africa, then I will feel safe to assume that the American culture is what blacks practice. If anyone dares to tell me that hip hop is a part of our culture, then I'd rather that child not learn about it. Hip hop culture today is absolutely degrading and in no way does it connect us to Africa.

I'd much rather see that child have some opportunities to advance in the world that perhaps will only come to them because they are being raised by white people. I think that child would grow up knowing that they will be confronted with racism soon enough.

Whether the child learns now or later does not necessarily determine any outcome for that child's future. With all of the reminders that we give to our children about the injustices done to blacks, I have yet to see the benefits. This is why sadly, this book is being written.

Being the victim has gotten our people absolutely nowhere. Being a victim does not appear to produce the drive to do something positive to lift us out of our current situations that we claim makes us a victim. When one of our people are killed unjustly by law enforcement, we scream the victim roles loud enough to convince ourselves that it's appropriate, even necessary, to loot, burn down and totally destroy what little we have in our own communities.

We take away more money from our people by destroying the few businesses that are owned by hard working black citizens. We actually wonder why America looks at blacks like they are insane? The act of constant destruction of your own backyard as a means to seek revenge on an outsider is completely INSANE. There's no other way to slice the pie on that one.

Stop looking for opportunities to play the poor little black victim. Stop comparing our history to the history of others. They were all atrocities. Stop getting angry at them. Stop insulting all of the people who actually were victims of lynching, shootings, being burned alive, having dogs set on them, rape, and imprisonment, so that we may become integrated, by trying to segregate ourselves all over again out of anger.

To me that is an enormous insult to our former civil rights leaders and our enslaved ancestors. We do not have the right to even voice our opinions because of anything we did. We have the right to voice our opinion because of THEM. To try to segregate our people all over again after all the deaths that occurred trying to integrate society, is a complete insult and leaves their deaths in vain.

Enough is enough already!

Chapter 11
Stop Enabling Our Men to Act Like Women

It appears to be some trend of some sort to feminize our men. Suddenly I see the young boys and the older men dressing like females and behaving more feminine than a female. This is a good way to start the extermination process. This is a very serious problem in so many ways and the issue cannot afford to be overlooked.

From the television shows to the big screen and all of the magazines and music in between, black men are assuming the female role at an alarming and disturbing rate.

Since when is it appropriate for men to wear grape skin tight jeans which somehow they manage to still sag? When has it become appropriate for men to carry purses and walk with a strong feminine switch? When we support celebrities and television shows that promote this nonsense, we are helping with the extermination process of our people.

Ladies, we may not realize it; but we contribute a great deal to this problem, unfortunately. Men have a particular role that he is supposed to and is expected to assume in the family. Men are supposed to be the providers. Unless there is a medical issue or other legitimate issue that hinders the man's ability to provide financially for his family, the man is expected to assume his position with pride.

Ladies, there seems to be a surge in role reversals lately. More and more of our men are at home "playing" babysitter while the women are at work, at school or both. These men show their dedication and support by getting up in the morning and starting the car for the wife or the "wifey" as many call their long time live-in girlfriends whom they have no real intentions of marrying. Or they lovingly drive these women to work and then drive the car around all day doing nothing but cheating, hanging out with the fellas, selling drugs, or going back home to play video games.

The sad thing about it is that a lot of these men refuse to put in the full time hours of the stay at home dad job that mothers put in. The home is not clean. Dinner is not cooked. The children are unattended and homework is not complete. On top of it all, these men have another person on the side many times. They use all of the woman's hard earned money to drink and smoke and go out.

But the worst part of all of this is that we enable these men by supporting them. They make a million promises to get a job. They have your car all day long and don't submit a single application, or if they do they never follow through with the status of the application. These men move into the woman's home. These men have absolutely nothing to show for themselves.

Ladies, please beware of any man still staying at home

with his parents that has no car, no job, and a bunch of excuses. We need to demand that our men actually man up and take care of our homes. It is not appropriate for a woman to have to work two and sometimes three jobs to cover the living expenses when there is a man involved. It is repulsive to see a woman working every day and barely meeting the bills while there is a healthy man sitting on the couch eating food that he purchased on the food stamp card.

Our sons are looking at this behavior. We raise our boys to live in a perpetual state of laziness and welfare dependent.

Women, we are not fathers. We are mothers, for those that have children. Why have we become so comfortable playing the role of the father when we aren't equipped to do so? Why would some women prefer to collect a child support check but not allow these men to actually take an active part in raising their children?

We are contributing to the downfall of these men. We are allowing them to relieve themselves from their roles as men. Women, we cannot raise men to be the sort of men they are supposed to be. We teach them how to be affectionate. We teach them how to nurture. We teach them about all of the things that make a woman happy. We show them the importance of taking time to look good.

Then they grow up. And they leave the home. The men are now equipped to be better women than the wonderful women who raised them. The things needed to be a man were never taught to them because some things only a man can teach a man.

Our men are supposed to be affectionate. They are supposed to know what makes a woman happy. This is how a good man learns to treat and keep his woman. But there is an enormous difference between teaching our men how to treat a woman and teaching our men how to be a woman.

These men are way too soft these days. They lack leadership and ambition. Accepting this new trend of men dressing like women is disgusting. Even if a man is a homosexual, that is his personal business - this does not make you any less of a male. You still have a penis even if you like penises for pleasure.

You are not a woman. And until we start allowing our men to be responsible for their roles as men, we are contributing to the extermination of our people. Until we stop supporting television shows, music, and any other entity that supports the effemination of our men, all for the sake of a dollar, we are contributing to the extermination of our people.

Chapter 12

Use Your History to Empower, Not to Enslave

When we think of the history of blacks we usually have images of slavery as the immediate thought. We need to start reminding ourselves of the history that teaches triumph after trials.

We need to feed ourselves with the history that forces us into the mindset of success instead of slavery. Viewing images of slaves hanging from trees and being beaten, is not going to put anyone into a success driven frame of mind. It will make people angry and it will keep the ball of anger rolling.

When you look at Oprah Winfrey, what are the odds that slavery will come to mind? No matter what some may think of her personally, success usually comes to everyone's mind. When you think of Betty Shabazz, Coretta Scott King, Angela Davis, Maya Angelou, Michelle Obama, Barack Obama, and Muhammad Ali, just to name a small fraction of people; shouldn't those names bring some level of pride to you?

If you were to ask any of these people what they want any memory of them to be, do you think anyone would want to bring to mind slavery?

Negro Colored Black African OH THE SHAME!

Instead of always remembering the part of history that degraded and victimized our people, start remembering the parts of history that should bring pride to the average mind. When these people went through their personal struggles to get to their height of achievement, they did not get there by using slavery as an excuse. They did not get there by allowing the victim role to take over their minds. They certainly did not get there by knocking each other down.

The truth is that the more we remind the world of the past the more they hate us. The truth is that reminding the world of the past is actually making us hate ourselves more. How can you begin to love yourself when the only thing you can equate with being black is being a slave? How can you expect to achieve and rise above the waters when you think that all we are good for are being slaves?

The more we remind the world that we were slaves the more everyone will see us as slaves. We will be treated as slaves. We will be respected as slaves. We will be hired as slaves. We will be expected to perform and to behave as slaves. This is what it means when people say, "GET OVER SLAVERY!"

It does not mean that you are ignoring the past. It does not make you a coon. It does not mean you are blinded. You are not a so-called negropean, as our people like to call black folks simply trying to get ahead. You are not a sellout. YOU ARE NOT A SLAVE. YOU ARE NOT A VICTIM.

You love your blackness enough place it on a pedestal of greatness and not slavery. You respect the abilities of your people to associate them and yourself with being achievers and not slaves.

NO ONE FEELS SORRY FOR YOU. GET OVER SLAVERY!

When people sincerely care, they often say things that may be undesirable to the ears. Those are the ones you may want to listen to. The words I just spoke and shouted are out of love.

This mentality that we have is doing nothing but contributing to our very own destruction. We stay angry. We look outside of ourselves to find something to complete ourselves.

If a person believes he is stupid, he will behave stupidly. If a person thinks he is ugly, he will walk about in shame because he thinks that he is ugly. If a person thinks he is not capable of great things, he will not try to be great because he doesn't think he has the capability.

All of these things are fed to individuals. If someone is constantly telling a person that they are stupid, ugly, or incapable of greatness, these things will shape the way a person behaves, the way he interacts with others, and the way that others will also treat him. So, if all you can think about is slavery when you think of being a black person, you will behave as a slave, a victim, you will treat others in society the way that you feel about yourself, and in turn they will treat you accordingly.

Negro Colored Black African OH THE SHAME!

GET OVER SLAVERY.

Google is your best friend. Feed your mind with positive thoughts of black history. Look up all of the inventors, the doctors, the lawyers. Look at the young black men and women graduating from medical school and law school now.

Listen to some jazz by famous black artists. Don't know of any? I recommend you get the book *Best of the Best Modern Jazz Recordings The Definitive Guide*, by K. Kelly McElroy.

Not a jazz fan? Listen to some oldies. Feed your mind with positive contributions of and for black people. Listen to music that soothes and doesn't degrade and disrespect our people. Just because it's trending - it doesn't make it right.

Chapter 13
HIV and AIDS is Very Real!

This subject affects everyone no matter what ethnic background and culture that you come from or identify with. For the sake of the subject of this book, however, we will speak about this issue as it pertains to Blacks.

We have a serious issue here. We have way too many of our brothers incarcerated.

During their incarceration these men have sexual relations among each other. Many of them then reenter into society with AIDS or a lot reenter into society as homosexuals and contract AIDS on the streets. They then go home to the girlfriend or wife and spread death unto her.

Know who you are sleeping with. Learn the history of the people, both men and women that you sleep with. It is impossible to know every single detail of an individual's sexual history. However, looking at behavioral patterns from their past and present may help you to gain some perspective. It is very important to take the time to know the person that you choose to lay with because this can be a death sentence.

Using protection is great but simply not enough. We live in a society of hypersexual beings. Everything that we are exposed to, from the liquor store advertisements, to the magazines on the newsstands, and especially the music videos and television programs; sex seems to be the focal point. Sex is idolized.

No one has self-control because society glorifies sexual promiscuity. This is not just something that men do. Women are catching up with the men now. A lot of women become frustrated because it seems that men have been unfaithful to women since the beginning of time and no matter what the woman has done to please her man, no matter how beautiful and exciting she is, men never seemed satisfied.

So now we have a generation of women paying this behavior forward back to men. We have a generation of very bitter and angry women who have vowed to return the cheating ways of men to our men. The scary part is that women are really starting not to care.

This behavior is a true way to exterminate our people. More and more people have become very comfortable "going raw" or not using condoms. They want to get the full effect. You still have many homes full of married couples or exclusive relationships where one partner is leading a double life. You have a society that encourages people to get their sexual needs met outside of their relationships whenever their needs are not being met at home. You ultimately have a society that encourages pleasure and living life to the fullest over responsibility and self-control!

According to the Center for Disease Control, in 2014

black men made up 70 percent of the new cases among blacks. Seventy percent of HIV cases were among black men. Please try to wrap your brain around that figure for just a second. Now multiply this times the amount of women that these men are sleeping with and you have a very scary situation that too many ignore until they get sick.

Contrary to popular belief, HIV is contracted more through heterosexual sex for the reason I mentioned earlier. There are too many brothers sleeping with men. There are too many brothers who used to sleep with men. Either way, they have sex with women and this is how it spreads so rapidly through heterosexual contact.

There is also the issue of drug abuse and sharing needles. This behavior was really popular in the Seventies through the Nineties. Don't forget that this was one of the major ways that HIV and AIDS were being spread among our people. If a person was a former drug user who shared needles remember that they could have contracted this disease years ago and have it show up later. HIV can live in the system without being detected for years which is why it is so important to get tested every six months.

People, you cannot have it both ways. You cannot be promiscuous and expect not to get burned. At some point each individual needs to decide which one is more important, sexual gratification for moments at a time or your life.

Men and women both need to stop cheating. If you have

multiple partners, use protection and still get tested regularly.

ANYONE who is married needs to be FAITHFUL. If you are so unsatisfied inside of your marriage that you feel like you must step outside of it to be happy, it is better to say goodbye, get a divorce, and at least let your spouse live instead of cheating and bringing all kinds of STD's back to your spouse and any children you bring into the world.

Anyone in an exclusive relationship should be sure that it is actually exclusive. Again, if you feel the need to step outside of your relationship you need to let your partner know BEFORE you act upon your impulses so that they may have a fair chance to decide what they want to do.

We cannot control the actions of others. People will continue to sleep around and unfortunately people will continue to cheat. This is why individual responsibility is paramount. It is the duty of every individual to do what is correct to keep ourselves protected.

The number of HIV cases among blacks is astronomical. Morality seems to be something frowned upon these days. So know your worth. Do not stay in relationships where the other individual is willing to risk the health of both you and themselves for something that they should love you enough to share exclusively with you.

Do not accept anyone who does not meet your moral standards. This is not being mean or overly picky. This is being smart. You have to be picky in order to ensure that you are getting what you deserve. We need to see these numbers of not only HIV and AIDS but other STD's drop drastically.

Let us not continue to contribute to the extermination of our own people.

Chapter 14
Going Back to Africa

After all of the talk about skin color, hatred for those who are light verses those who are dark, and all the problems in our communities that come along with this sad subject of skin color, the truth is that every human being on the planet is somehow traced back to Africa.

It doesn't matter how minuscule the drop of blood is, the fact of the matter is that humanity began in Africa. Yes even our fellow white people are from Africa.

Take a look at Africa. What do you see? How many people who call themselves African Americans can actually tell anyone something significant about Africa? During Black History month, instead of recalling all of the lynching, beatings, slavery and other forms of torture and murder, why not take a journey back to Africa. There is no excuse not to be able to learn countless things about the beauty in Africa.

What makes a child so excited to use crayons? Honestly, it's not the white or the black crayon, it's the colored crayons. Negro and black are colors. They are a figurative representation of the darkest skin colors. White is a color. Again it is a figurative representation of the lightest skin

Negro Colored Black African OH THE SHAME!

colors.

I have indeed seen people who have blue black skin and even underneath the black there lies a beautiful blue undertone. Blue people are what I like to refer to them as. Blue is one of my personal favorite colors.

Africa has all shades from the lightest of light to the darkest of dark. People of Africa have all hair types and all types of facial features. Dark and ugly seems to be the way we associate people with Africa. Somehow dark seems to be a curse word in America.

If you speak to someone from Africa you will see that they equate dark skin with royalty. They equate broad noses and full lips with strength. Too many people fear any close connection to Africa because they automatically envision slave ships and captivity.

Ignorance is not bliss.

Again I must say that our people need to stop feeding their minds with the slavery that happened in the past. It cheapens the lives and hard work put forth by every colored person who fought for every shade of brown to have the same rights as those with pink skin. It stirs up feelings of weakness, fear, and intimidation among those who somehow feel that slaves were weak.

Don't forget that even the brown shades from Africa participated in slavery. Also remember that slavery is history, but it is not your history or my history. Slavery never happened to us.

The only slavery that is happening today is the type that we create in our own minds. Our people have become slaves to spending money. Our people have become slaves to anger and bitterness. If you truly want to be free, take the time to actually seek beauty and go back to Africa to find it.

Start visiting Africa by reading about it. Watch the positive documentaries. Most of all remember that the one thing that our friends and enemies alike have in common is Africa.

Chapter 15

It Takes a Village

Single parent households seem to be the norm in our communities. This generation coming up is scary to me. These are the children that we will have to rely upon to care for us when we grow old. The children have absolutely no respect for their elders. Gone are the days when communities helped each other to rear our children and not only teach them respect, but also to enforce it.

When I was a child we held the doors open for our elders. We offered to carry groceries home for free for our elders. When our parents were having a conversation, not only did we not interrupt them; we left the area. Young people really didn't speak a bunch to adults unless we were spoken to. We understood the serious consequences of raising our voices or being sassy to our elders when they told us to do something.

We also took dinner time a lot more seriously. Families sat at a table over a home cooked meal and the parents actually talked to their kids about what happened for the day.

Children did not have all of the distractions of technology that the kids of this generation have, so we were forced to use our imaginations. Our parents taught us to never use the word bored. We played outdoors and created all kinds of things to do. Children played together quite nicely because families were much more structured in my generation.

When we did fight, we fought fair. More than likely no one would shoot you just for looking at them wrong or saying something to them.

There is no way that we would have gotten away with wearing our pants below our bottoms at all, let alone in front of our parents, our elders, and at school. Our parents actually took the time to make sure that our clothing was age appropriate. Our parents were not hell bent on trying to be our friends. They were our parents and we had a healthy fear of them.

The kids of this generation think that they are entitled to whatever they want. These kids also carry guns like we carried backpacks. They are heartless and they lack any remorse for anything they do. Instead of trying to help by calling for help when an assault is being witnessed, they video record the assault on their phones and post it to social media for entertainment.

What really bothers me is that the parents seem to have forgotten the morals of the generation we grew up in and they are just as bad as their kids these days.

Parents are either too busy trying to keep the bills paid, to actually watch their children or they are too busy having their adult fun to watch their children.

Nowadays if a neighbor told a child to do something, they may get shot. People are too afraid to say something to these kids. That's the problem. There are no consequences for these children today.

Our people will never progress and our communities will never be safe if we fail to raise our children properly. These kids walk around and talk about all of the horrible racism they have to experience each day and then they turn around and shoot one of their own people, with a smile on their faces.

The children have become the parents and the parents have become almost absent. Young boys look to celebrities that degrade women and insult our people because fathers are not around to teach them any differently.

Young girls look to these over sexualized images of women as a guide to who and how they should be because their mothers are either too busy being mom and dad and trying to work two and three jobs to keep the bills paid or the moms are putting sorry men before their children.

It starts at home. Again, we can't control other people's children any more than we can control adults. But we can control our home and how we raise our children.

If more people put the effort forth to start putting fear back into these children, our communities would become noticeably safer and stronger.

Negro Colored Black African OH THE SHAME!

We need to go back to old school. Begin with your own home. Make your home is the village that it takes to raise your children.

Chapter 16
At the End of the Day

Create your own happiness. We live in a world where people will hate you because of your skin color. People will judge you based upon your ethnicity. Some people may have more extended to them than the next.

These are facts and you can count on these things happening just like taxes and death.

There is one thing that no one can take from you unless you give them the power to:

They cannot take your mind.

Self-hatred is taught. Unlearn any hatred that you have for yourself. There is no such thing as black pride or African pride if you don't have self-pride. You cannot think that Black is beautiful if you don't think that you are beautiful. You cannot boast about wearing your natural hair if you think that nappy hair is bad hair. You will continue to perpetuate the hatred, division and stereotypes for as long as you continue to accept the present degenerative state of being that our people are living in today.

At the end of the day, in order to be happy you must create your own happiness because no one is responsible

Negro Colored Black African OH THE SHAME!

for your happiness except for you. In order to be able to create your own happiness you must be able to accept that it is no longer the white man's fault. You must know that you are capable of doing anything that you set your mind to. You must stop equating Negro Colored Black and African with slavery. Realize that you are not a slave nor were you ever.

No one owes black people anything. Black people are not some special case that is entitled to reparations or public apologies. Start creating a more positive history for black people so that when our grandchildren have children, they can celebrate our history by telling them about all of the black people who became great doctors and lawyers and scientists and professors. Show them a history of rebuilding our people from the perilous state that we live in now.

If nothing else in this book means anything to anyone, I pray that these final words will hit home and touch your heart. Rip this chapter out of the book! Make copies of it and pass it along to any and every individual that you see. Let's not just talk about it - let's enforce it!

When we see one another let us say hello instead of walking past with an evil look. When someone is starting a business, support them. Stop trying to out-do one another. Contributing to the well-being of yourself will enable you to contribute to the well-being of the black communities.

Unlearn that **NEGRO** equals weak. Unlearn that **COLORED** equals segregation. Unlearn that **BLACK** equals ugly. Unlearn that **AFRICAN** equals slavery and shame.

RITCHIE MAC

One Love!

About the Author

Ritchie Mac is a non-fictional, no nonsense, author who addresses the issues that affect all people from all walks of life, with the goal of resolution in all matters where resolution may be possible.

Negro Colored Black African

OH THE SHAME!

RITCHIE MAC

Freedom Underground Publishing

www.ingramcontent.com/pod-product-compliance
Lightning Source LLC
Chambersburg PA
CBHW071315040426
42444CB00009B/2024